GET THE ANSWERS! **History**

Q&A ABOUT THE U.S. CONSTITUTION

By Benjamin Proudfit

INVESTIGATE!

Enslow PUBLISHING

Please visit our website, www.enslow.com. For a free color catalog of all our high-quality books, call toll free 1-800-398-2504 or fax 1-877-980-4454.

Library of Congress Cataloging-in-Publication Data

Names: Proudfit, Benjamin, author.
Title: Q & A about the U.S. Constitution / Benjamin Proudfit.
Other titles: Questions and answers about the United States Constitution
Description: Buffalo, New York : Enslow Publishing, 2026. | Series: Get the answers! History | Includes index. | Audience: Grades 2-3
Identifiers: LCCN 2024061274 (print) | LCCN 2024061275 (ebook) | ISBN 9781978544468 (library binding) | ISBN 9781978544451 (paperback) | ISBN 9781978544475 (ebook)
Subjects: LCSH: United States. Constitution–Juvenile literature.
Classification: LCC E303 .P93 2026 (print) | LCC E303 (ebook) | DDC 342.7302/9–dc23/eng/20250213
LC record available at https://lccn.loc.gov/2024061274
LC ebook record available at https://lccn.loc.gov/2024061275

Published in 2026 by
Enslow Publishing
2544 Clinton Street
Buffalo, NY 14224

Copyright © 2026 Enslow Publishing

Designer: Andrea Davison-Bartolotta
Editor: Kristen Nelson

Photo credits: Cover, pp. 1, 9, 15, 20, 24 Library of Congress; series art (question mark backgrounds) Darcraft/Shutterstock.com; p. 4 Brian A Jackson/Shutterstock.com; p. 5 Dennis MacDonald/Shutterstock.com; p. 6 Consolidated News Photos/Shutterstock.com; p. 7 National Archives; p. 8 File:Congress voting independence.jpg/Wikimedia Commons; pp. 10, 19, 21, 22 National Portrait Gallery, Smithsonian Institution; p. 11 (Madison) Prachaya Roekdeethaweesab/Shutterstock.com; p. 11 (chart) bsd studio/Shutterstock.com; p. 12 ungvar/Shutterstock.com; p. 13 Maria_Ermolenko/Shutterstock.com; pp. 14, 17 mark reinstein/Shutterstock.com; p. 16 Tada Images/Shutterstock.com; p. 18 Studio Romantic/Shutterstock.com; p. 23 Everett Collection/Shutterstock.com; p. 26 Collection of the Supreme Court of the United States; p. 27 christianthiel.net/Shutterstock.com; p. 28 Benjamin Clapp/Shutterstock.com; p. 29 AVAVA/Shutterstock.com.

All rights reserved. No part of this book may be reproduced in any form without permission in writing from the publisher, except by a reviewer.

Printed in the United States of America

Some of the images in this book illustrate individuals who are models. The depictions do not imply actual situations or events.

CPSIA compliance information: Batch #CS26ENS: For further information contact Enslow Publishing, at 1-800-398-2504.

CONTENTS

An Old Document 4
The First Constitution 6
Writing the Constitution. 9
What Does It Say? 12
In Favor and Against 19
Constitution Changes and Challenges 23
Written to Last 28
Glossary 30
For More Information 31
Index 32

Words in the glossary appear in **bold** type the first time they are used in the text.

AN OLD DOCUMENT

The U.S. Constitution was written more than 230 years ago. The United States was a young country when this **document** was written. The 13 states had only won their independence from Great Britain a few years before!

In the United States, the Constitution is the highest law. All other laws, including those passed in states, need to agree with it. It can be amended, or changed, but it isn't easy to do that. What do you want to know about the U.S. Constitution?

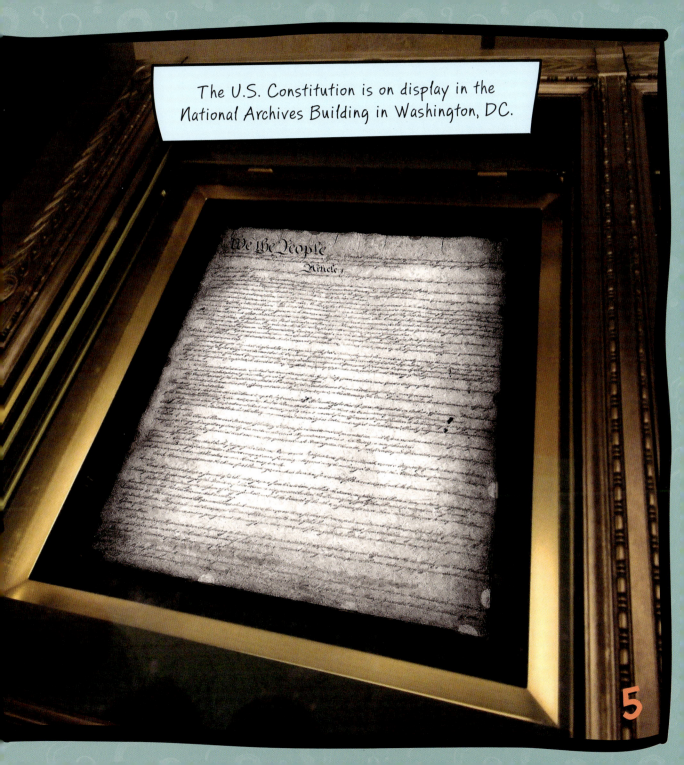

The U.S. Constitution is on display in the National Archives Building in Washington, DC.

THE FIRST CONSTITUTION

QUESTION 1

Why write a constitution?

ANSWER

A constitution sets up how a government will run and the leaders within the government. It lists the basic laws of a country. It also establishes the **relationship** between a government and citizens.

President Joe Biden

The ideas included in a country's constitution are the **foundation** on which a country is built.

QUESTION 2

What were the Articles of Confederation?

••••• **ANSWER** •••••

The Articles were the first constitution that governed the United States! They went into effect in March 1781. The Articles unified the 13 British colonies into 13 states. In fact, the Articles named the new country the United States of America!

Confederation means to come together or be united.

QUESTION 3

Why don't the Articles govern the United States today?

ANSWER

The Articles had many problems. For example, the central government was too weak. The one house of Congress had no authority over the states and could not collect taxes. The new government was in trouble!

The United States was governed by the Articles while it fought the end of the American Revolution, the war in which the country won its freedom from Great Britain, and into its first years as a nation.

WRITING THE CONSTITUTION

QUESTION 4

What happened at the Constitutional Convention?

ANSWER

Representatives from each state—except Rhode Island—met in Philadelphia, Pennsylvania, beginning in May 1787 to fix the problems with the Articles. Soon they realized a new constitution was needed. They started working on one!

The Constitutional Convention met in the Pennsylvania State House, now called Independence Hall.

QUESTION 5

Who wrote the Constitution?

ANSWER

Many Founding Fathers attended the Constitutional Convention and gave input for the final document. James Madison, a representative from Virginia, is called the "father of the Constitution." He put forth the idea of three branches of government that make up the U.S. government!

Benjamin Franklin was the oldest **delegate** at the convention. His ideas commanded a lot of respect.

The Three Branches of Government

Legislative Branch

makes laws; includes the two houses of Congress, the Senate and the House of Representatives

• • •

Executive Branch

carries out laws; led by the president

• • •

Judicial Branch

interprets laws; includes the courts

• • •

The U.S. Constitution outlines three branches of government: the executive branch, the legislative branch, and the judicial branch. This was Madison's idea!

11

WHAT DOES IT SAY?

QUESTION 6

What is the preamble?

ANSWER

It's the first part of the Constitution. It's only 52 words! The preamble introduces the document and gives the Constitution's basic goals. It starts with: "We the People of the United States."

There are seven articles, or parts, that follow the preamble in the U.S. Constitution.

QUESTION 7

What does Article I say?

ANSWER

Article I sets up the legislative branch, Congress. It says how people can be **elected** as senators and representatives. It also lists the powers of Congress, including its ability to collect taxes.

Today, both houses of Congress meet in the U.S. Capitol building in Washington, DC.

QUESTION 8

Is the president in the Constitution?

••••• ANSWER •••••

Yes! Article II sets up the executive branch led by the president. It establishes how the president is elected and how they may be removed. It lists the president's powers, such as being the commander in chief of the U.S. armed forces.

According to Article II, the president may **appoint** people to certain government positions. Congress then has to agree to these appointments.

President Bill Clinton

QUESTION 9

Did the Constitution set up the Supreme Court?

••••• **ANSWER** •••••

Article III establishes a judicial branch, including **federal** courts headed by "one supreme Court." However, this article is much more general than Articles I and II. The Judiciary Law of 1789 is what truly set up how the courts would work.

JUSTICES OF THE SUPREME COURT OF THE UNITED STATES

Members of the Supreme Court are called justices. They know a lot about the Constitution!

15

QUESTION 10

What is a "republican form of government"?

••••• **ANSWER** •••••

It's not explained in the Constitution! The part of Article IV that promises this kind of government is called the Guarantee **Clause**. It generally means the people have a say in how they are governed and who governs.

U.S. citizens have their say in government by voting.

QUESTION 11

Can the Constitution be changed?

ANSWER

Yes, and Article V outlines the ways the Constitution can be amended. Once an amendment passes, it becomes part of the Constitution. An amendment can be proposed, or put forth, in Congress or at a convention called by the states.

All proposed amendments have to be **ratified** by three-fourths of states to become part of the Constitution.

U.S. Congress

QUESTION 12

What is the Supremacy Clause?

ANSWER

It's the part of Article VI that says federal laws are the highest in the land. It solved a problem from the time under the Articles. State courts weren't looking to federal laws when deciding some cases. The Supremacy Clause made it clear they should be.

IN FAVOR AND AGAINST

QUESTION 13

Who were the Federalists?

ANSWER

They were the group of leaders who supported the ratification of the new U.S. Constitution. They believed the strong national government it included was needed to build a great nation.

One of the loudest voices among the Federalists was Alexander Hamilton. He became the first secretary of the treasury.

QUESTION 14

What were The Federalist Papers?

ANSWER

These 85 essays argued in favor of ratifying the new Constitution. They were printed in newspapers in New York. Hamilton wrote 51, Madison wrote 29, and John Jay wrote 5.

> Hamilton, Madison, and Jay wrote The Federalist Papers under the name "Publius."

20

Question 15

Who were the Anti-Federalists?

ANSWER

This group of leaders did not want the Constitution to be ratified. They thought the document gave the central government too much power. They wanted the states to be more powerful in the new nation.

Anti-Federalists, like Patrick Henry, wanted a list of rights, or freedoms, guaranteed to citizens included in the U.S. Constitution—especially if the national government was going to be strong.

Patrick Henry

QUESTION 16

When was the Constitution ratified?

ANSWER

Nine of the 13 states had to ratify the Constitution in order for it to go into effect. This happened on June 21, 1788, when New Hampshire ratified the document. However, Rhode Island didn't ratify the Constitution until 1790!

George Washington was elected the first president under the U.S. Constitution. He served from 1789 to 1797.

CONSTITUTION CHANGES AND CHALLENGES

QUESTION 17

What is the Bill of Rights?

ANSWER

The first 10 amendments to the Constitution are known together as the Bill of Rights. They list the rights guaranteed, or promised, to all U.S. citizens. These include the freedom of speech, the right to **due process**, freedom of assembly, and many more.

Madison wrote the Bill of Rights. He first wrote 17 amendments. Ten made it through Congress and state ratification.

23

QUESTION 18

Are there other amendments?

ANSWER

Including the Bill of Rights, there are 27 amendments total. The 13th Amendment abolished, or ended slavery in the United States. It was ratified in December 1865 shortly after the end of the **American Civil War**.

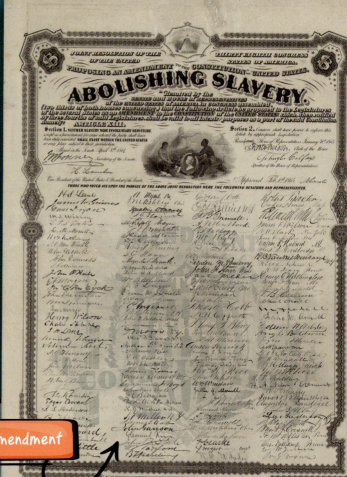

resolution proposing the 13th amendment

Major Amendments

1791 — The first 10 amendments to the Constitution are ratified.

1865 — The 13th Amendment abolishes slavery.

1868 — The 14th Amendment makes everyone born in the United States citizens, including those who were formerly enslaved.

1870 — The 15th Amendment gives all men the right to vote.

1920 — The 19th Amendment gives all U.S. citizens, including women, the right to vote.

1951 — The 22nd Amendment limits the number of terms a president can serve to two.

1971 — The 26th Amendment sets the national voting age at 18.

> About 11,000 amendments to the Constitution have been proposed and only 27 have made it through to ratification!

QUESTION 19

What does "unconstitutional" mean?

ANSWER

This means something doesn't agree with the Constitution. It could be a law passed by a town or state or the action of the president or other government official. Part of the Supreme Court's job is to decide cases that have to do with questions of constitutionality.

Supreme Court justices serve for life.

QUESTION 20

Will the Constitution ever be replaced?

ANSWER

As of right now, there isn't a large movement to get rid of the U.S. Constitution. In fact, it hasn't even been amended since 1992! However, there are always groups finding new ways to challenge this founding document.

WRITTEN TO LAST

The U.S. Constitution has been around for a long time! It continues to guide how the U.S. government runs even though life today is much different than it was in the late 1700s.

People still spend a lot of time interpreting and studying the Constitution today. Not everyone agrees about what it says. Still, the U.S. Constitution has withstood these disagreements and other tests of time—and will continue to!

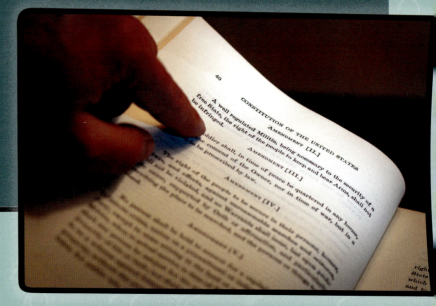

GLOSSARY

American Civil War: A war fought from 1861 to 1865 in the United States between the Union (the Northern states) and the Confederacy (the Southern states).

appoint: To name to a position.

clause: A part of a legal document.

delegate: A representative of one of the 13 colonies.

document: A formal piece of writing.

due process: Laws or steps to follow to be sure people are treated fairly when they may have done something wrong.

elect: To choose for a position in a government.

federal: Having to do with the national government.

foundation: A not-for-profit organization provided with funds to support charitable works.

interpret: To explain the meaning of.

ratify: To give formal approval to something.

relationship: A connection between two things.

representative: A person who stands for a group of people.

FOR MORE INFORMATION

BOOKS

Gottlieb, Beth. *Who Wrote the Constitution?* Buffalo, New York: Gareth Stevens Publishing, 2026.

Latta, Sara L. *History Tipsters Break Down the U.S. Constitution: The Inside Scoop on Our Founding Document.* North Mankato, MN: Capstone Press, 2024.

WEBSITES

Constitutions | Social Studies Shorts
https://thinktv.pbslearningmedia.org/resource/constitutions-video/social-studies-shorts/
Watch a short video about constitutions, the U.S. Constitution, and what an amendment is.

U.S. Constitution: 1789
https://bensguide.gpo.gov/u-s-constitution-1789
Check out this kid friendly look at the Constitution.

Publisher's note to educators and parents: Our editors have carefully reviewed these websites to ensure that they are suitable for students. Many websites change frequently, however, and we cannot guarantee that a site's future contents will continue to meet our high standards of quality and educational value. Be advised that students should be closely supervised whenever they access the internet.

INDEX

amendments, 17, 23, 24, 25

American Revolution, 8

Anti-Federalists, 21

Articles of Confederation, 7, 8, 18

articles of the Constitution, 13, 14, 15, 16, 17, 18

branches of government, 10, 11

Bill of Rights, 23, 24

Congress, 8, 11, 13, 14, 17, 23

Constitutional Convention, 9, 10

Federalists, 19, 20

Federalist Papers, The, 20

Franklin, Benjamin, 10

Guarantee Clause, 16

Hamilton, Alexander, 19, 20

Henry, Patrick, 21

Madison, James, 10, 20, 23

preamble, 12

president, 11, 14, 22, 25, 26

ratification, 17, 19, 21, 22, 23, 24, 25

states, 4, 7, 8, 17, 21, 22

Supremacy Clause, 18

Supreme Court, 14, 26

unconstitutional, 26

U.S. Capitol building, 13

Washington, DC, 5, 13

Washington, George, 22